Glacier National Park is a haven for some 2,000 mountain goats, residents of the alpine meadows and mountain summits which dominate the park. Keen brown eyes scan the sky-high splendor that is Glacier, but the park is more than just a pretty view. A variety of weather and landscape yields a splendid diversity of wildlife in this national park astride the Continental Divide.

*M*eadows full of beargrass blossoms turn
Glacier visitors into wildflower enthusiasts.
Here forest flowers meet alpine tundra relatives,
and prairie flowers mix with native plants of the
Rocky Mountains to create an unparalleled
display of abundant beauty.

Front cover: Going-to-the-Sun Road in the shadow of Mount Clements, photo by Brett Baunton. Inside front cover: Waterton River near Goat Haunt in Glacier, photo by Gary Ladd. Page 1: Mountain goat, photo by Irene Hinke-Sacilotto. Pages 2/3: Beargrass at Logan Pass, photo by Ed Cooper. Pages 4/5: Moonrise over the Continental Divide, photo by George Wuerthner.

Glacier National Park, located in northwestern Montana on the Canadian border, was established in 1910. Canada and the United States expanded the national park concept in 1932, when they formed Waterton-Glacier International Peace Park.

Edited by Cheri C. Madison.
Book design by K. C. DenDooven.

Second Printing, 1995
in pictures GLACIER The Continuing Story.
© 1993 KC PUBLICATIONS, INC.
LC 93-77022. ISBN 0-88714-067-X.

in pictures
Glacier

by Cindy Nielsen

The Continuing Story®

Cindy Nielsen began her National Park Service career in 1972. She holds two M.S. Degrees from the University of Wyoming—one in Parks & Recreation Management and one in Natural Sciences. Her work as a national park naturalist has led her from the Rocky Mountains to the desert of Death Valley and the underwater kelp forest of Channel Islands. Cindy has been at Glacier since 1989.

ED COOPER

National park areas are special landscapes set aside by acts of Congress to protect and preserve features of national significance that are generally categorized as scenic, scientific, historical, and recreational.

As Americans, we are joint caretakers of these unique places, and we gladly share them with visitors from around the world.

George Bird Grinnell christened Glacier the "Crown of the Continent" when he visited the region at the turn of the twentieth century. Grinnell, an eclectic conservationist, founded both the Audubon Club and "Field and Stream" magazine. He was an early advocate for establishing Glacier as a national park. The alpine landscape Grinnell so admired began as ancient ocean sediments—uplifted as part of the Rocky Mountain cordillera and shaped by 2 million years of glacial erosion. Today, mountain meadows and evergreen forests soften the view near tree limit. Fifty small glaciers persist in the park as reminders of the erosive power of glacial ice.

Glaciers named Grinnell, Gem, and Salamander perch high on the headwall of Many Glacier Valley.

From Rock and Ice

Glacier National Park is not named for huge Ice Age glaciers. Only small alpine glaciers remain, dating from a little ice age less than 10,000 years ago. The park was named for its glaciated landscape, an awe-inspiring mix of deep glacial valleys, high bowl-shaped cirques, and sharply pointed peaks called horns, carved from sedimentary rocks laid down in an ancient ocean.

The glaciers which sculpted this landscape were often many thousands of feet thick, and their relentless erosive power profoundly altered the limestones, siltstones, and mudstones of the park. Like all glaciers, those of the Pleistocene or Ice Age formed when the climate in this region was several degrees cooler on average than it is now. During the Ice Age, summer was shorter and winter was longer. Then, as now, glaciers formed when more snow fell during the winter months than melted during the summer. The unmelted snow recrystallized; snowflakes lost their sharp edges and bonded together to form firn ice. Eventually enough ice accumulated and a glacier was born.

Movement defines a true glacier. Glacial ice flows for several reasons. The weight of a glacier deforms the ice like pressure on silly putty or jello, and the glacier flows downslope under the influence of gravity. Glaciers melt where ice rubs against rock, and the thin film of water created lubricates the body of the glacier so that it slides along. As the glacier moves it picks up rocks and grinds, scratches, and scours its path.

◀ **H**idden Lake lies at the bottom of a glacial cirque. A glacier once filled this rocky amphitheater. As the glacier flowed downhill, thawing and freezing water plucked rock from the surrounding mountain peaks and created this bowl-shaped cirque, a distinctive feature of alpine glaciers.

Grinnell Glacier and the long thin ▽ Salamander Glacier above were linked by an ice fall when George Bird Grinnell first visited in 1885. Since the turn of the century, half the glacier has melted away, yet it survives in the shade of the Garden Wall.

Ancient Oceans

Ripple marks are a common feature of the ▷
siltstones found throughout the park. Beginning
1.5 billion years ago, advancing and retreating seas
created a variety of sedimentary rock layers, some
deposited in shallow moving waters, others laid
down in the quiet depths of a deep ocean.

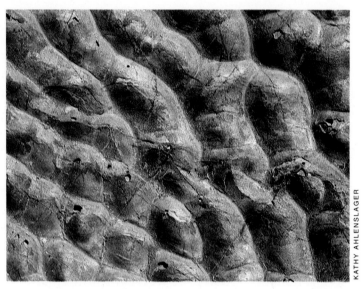

KATHY AHLENSLAGER

KATHY AHLENSLAGER

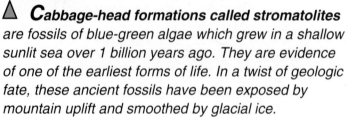

▲ **C**abbage-head formations called stromatolites
are fossils of blue-green algae which grew in a shallow
sunlit sea over 1 billion years ago. They are evidence
of one of the earliest forms of life. In a twist of geologic
fate, these ancient fossils have been exposed by
mountain uplift and smoothed by glacial ice.

Sedimentary rock layers and icy crevasses form ▷
parallel patterns at Jackson Glacier. Deep cracks called
crevasses form in the brittle blue surface when fast-
moving ice pulls apart. Ice on the surface of a glacier
cracks more easily than ice under pressure deep in the
moving glacier. The weight of surface layers compresses
the ice within the glacier so that it behaves like a liquid.
Even though Jackson Glacier continues to flow downhill,
it has been in retreat since 1860. The ice is melting faster
than the glacier can flow forward. Jackson Glacier has
lost about 75 percent of its surface area in this century,
an indication that the climate of the park is warmer than it
was 100 years ago.

Glaciers scoured ▷
off the edges of these
fossil ripple marks near
Sperry Glacier. Close
inspection reveals long
parallel scratches where
the surface has been
worn away. These glacial
striations result when
stones, frozen in the
base of a glacier, abrade
exposed bedrock as
glacial ice flows over
the surface.

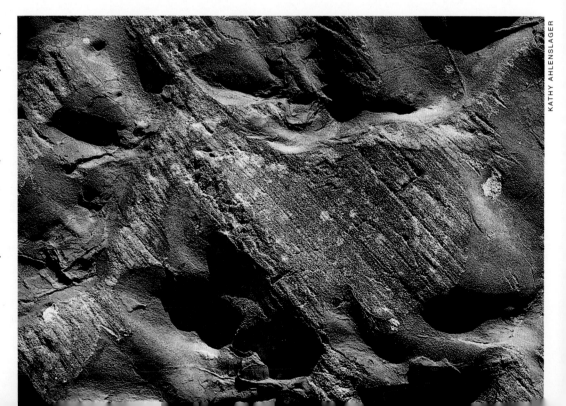

KATHY AHLENSLAGER

Glacial Evidence

⚠ **Broad U-shaped valleys are the signature of** a glaciated landscape. This valley, northwest of Two Medicine Pass, gives silent testimony to the carving power of an Ice Age glacier. Two million years ago, before the Ice Age began, this valley was probably V-shaped with steep sides and a narrow base. As the glacier flowed down the valley it acted not so much like a bulldozer, but rather like a conveyor belt, dislodging and picking up rocks and carrying them to the terminus of the ice. Today no remnant of Pleistocene ice remains, but snow lingers in the cirque near the head of the valley, ready to form another glacier if the climate cools again.

A chain of lakes illustrates beautiful but ▷ subtle evidence of glacial erosion. Grinnell Lake, in the foreground, receives a heavy load of tiny rock particles ground up by the moving ice of Grinnell Glacier. Milky glacial meltwater gives the lake its aquamarine hue. Light reflected from rock flour suspended in the water of Josephine Lake tints it an opalescent blue. Downstream in the distance, Sherburne Lake impounds the runoff of Many Glacier Valley but receives little rock flour to color its waters.

The Continental Divide lies along the
summits of the Lewis Range in the heart of
Glacier National Park. The name of the range
commemorates Captain Meriwether Lewis
who passed near the present-day park on his
expedition's return trip in 1805. Park
boundaries encompass 1 million acres of
wilderness. Class I air quality and visibility of
200 miles allow us to enjoy the view. Blackfeet
Indians called the high mountain vastness of
the park "The Backbone of the World."

◁ **Although political boundaries divide**
Canada and the United States, snow and rain
falling in Glacier feed the great river systems of
the entire North American continent. Nowhere is
this more striking than in southeastern Glacier
National Park at Triple Divide Peak. Here the
Continental Divide splits into three drainages
leading to the Pacific Ocean, the Gulf of Mexico,
and the Arctic via Hudson Bay.

NPS PHOTO

High Divides

Near Logan Pass ranks ▷ of evergreen forests slowly give way to rocky summits at tree limit. The horn of Mount Reynolds was shaped by powerful Pleistocene glaciers carving rock from its sides as they flowed into the valleys below. Snow and icy cold still shape both the landscape and the life which covers it. At this northern latitude trees seldom grow above 8,000 feet. Tree limit is a function of both latitude and elevation. Air is physically thinner at high elevations and less able to retain heat. Cold temperatures slow growth until, at highest elevations, only perennial grasses, specially adapted wildflowers, and lichens can sustain themselves. This alpine environment supports hardy but fragile life vulnerable to the impact of millions of park visitors. Regulations encourage hikers to stay on trails in order to preserve this alpine beauty for next season's visitors and for future generations.

PAT O'HARA

PAT O'HARA

▲ **The quiet waters of Hidden Lake mirror Bearhat Mountain, named for a Kootenai Indian leader.**
Bearhat's name was originally given to the lake, but many place-name changes were applied to park geography in the 1930s. The Kootenai, Salish, and Blackfeet names which label park features help visitors to recognize a long tradition of use by native peoples in this area. These names are not just historical footnotes, but reminders that dynamic native cultures continue to add diversity and meaning to the park.

IRENE HINKE-SACILOTTO

A Legacy of Lakes

LARRY BURTON

▲ **A**valanche Lake fills the basin of a large cirque quarried by an Ice Age glacier. In 1895, geologist Dr. Lyman Sperry named the lake and scaled the steep headwall beyond, where he first viewed the modern glacier which bears his name.

◄ **T**he snow-covered summit of Divide Mountain dominates the ridge of Hudson Bay Divide above St. Mary Lake. There are actually two St. Mary Lakes astride the eastern border of Glacier National Park. Upper St. Mary Lake, just inside the park boundary, drains into Lower St. Mary Lake on the Blackfeet Indian Reservation.

The Source

Water in all its forms—snow and avalanche, glaciers and meltwater, flooding creeks and placid lakes—continues to create the park anew each season. Over 80 inches of snow fall in the high country of the park each year. Winter winds build snow cornices which give way in spring to massive avalanches. Humans may regard avalanches as safety hazards or destructive inconveniences, but in the reality of nature an avalanche is a natural force which clears the steep slope and makes way for the huckleberry crop of the future.

Snow from Glacier National Park feeds the great river systems of North America. A snowflake falling on Mount Oberlin flows as meltwater into McDonald Creek and joins the Flathead River on its way to the mighty Columbia. The same storm will deposit snow on the roof of the Logan Pass Visitor Center, a mere mile away. This northbound snowflake will be captured by the St. Mary River and flow across Canada to Hudson Bay. Capricious winter winds will blow other snowflakes over the knife ridge of the Garden Wall just across the Going-to-the-Sun Road. There, in a north-facing cirque, lies Grinnell Glacier waiting to receive replenishing winter snow and incorporate the crystals into glacial ice. Finally, if the storm is a large one, snowflakes will fall on the southeast face of Triple Divide Peak, to join Atlantic Creek when summer sunshine prevails again.

The park is much more than snow, ice, and avalanche. Two hundred lakes shape the character of Glacier's wildlife and visitor experience. Power boats ply the waters of Lake McDonald, while only non-motorized craft are allowed on Kintla Lake. Most lakes are open to fishing, and cutthroat trout spawn here. Fishermen and lakeside cabins share the shoreline with nesting bald eagles and loons, and present a challenge to park managers who must preserve wildlife and provide for the enjoyment of the people.

ED COOPER

▲ *A winter sun shines weakly through the snow* in Many Glacier Valley. Winter lasts seven months or more in this part of the park. Mountain snows begin in earnest by October, but late storms in June and early storms in August are not unusual at higher elevations.

▲ *Grinnell Glacier is one of 50 small alpine glaciers in the park. It has lost much of its ice mass to a warm climate over the past century. Between 1937 and 1968, the glacier receded over 400 feet. The rapid retreat of Grinnell Glacier has left little time for soil formation and plant growth to soften the contours of this recently eroded landscape.*

The Big Drift on ▷ *Going-to-the-Sun Road surprises spring and summer visitors with its long life. In a typical season, it will be late August before this 70-foot-high drift will melt away. It is interesting to speculate what might happen if the climate began to cool once more. Would a new glacier form here?*

KATHY AHLENSLAGER

A Trickle or a Torrent

KATHY AHLENSLAGER

▲ **A**tsina Falls plunges over a cliff along the trail to Stoney Indian Pass. At the base of the cliff, large fan-shaped piles of rock called talus accumulate from yet another form of erosion. Cold overnight temperatures freeze meltwater as it seeps into cracks in the cliff face. As the water turns to ice, it expands and pops off chunks of rock, forming the talus slopes below.

▲ **A**ppekunny Falls cascades into Many Glacier Valley. A short steep trail of less than a mile climbs quickly to the falls. This hike is a favorite of early summer visitors. Its south-facing slope melts out early, well before other trails open up in the Many Glacier area.

The power of Swiftcurrent ▷
Creek carves a narrow path
through the rocks which form a
natural dam for Swiftcurrent Lake
just upstream.

▲ **"The musical tinkle of the tiny rivulet, the deep bass roar of the dashing torrent, the hiss of** *rushing water, confined as in a flume, fell upon the ear...."* — *from the diary of George Bird Grinnell, on his 1888 visit to what he called the St. Mary country and what would later become Glacier National Park. The torrent of Siyeh Creek is part of a 1,450-mile network of rivers and streams in Glacier National Park. As the creek rushes downslope it cuts ever deeper into layers of sedimentary rock uplifted as part of the Lewis Overthrust 60 million years ago.*

Toward the Sea

▲ **The placid waters of Two Medicine Lake reflect Mount Sinopah,** *named for the wife of trapper Hugh Monroe. Almost one-third of the park is covered by water. Indians and trappers first exploited the water's richness. Today visitors enjoy both quiet contemplation and motorized boats. And through it all, water continues to carry the mountains toward the sea.*

Overleaf: *It is easy to ▷ understand why the Blackfeet called this region around St. Mary Lake, "The Lakes Inside." Photo by Jeff Gnass.*

In a State of Nature

A 1910 Act of Congress preserved Glacier as "a public park...in a state of nature...for the care and protection of the fish and game within the boundaries." The birds and mammals of Glacier National Park are no longer called "game" because they are no longer hunted within this million-acre reserve. The founders of the park possessed a vision of preservation that went beyond the limits of 19th century vocabulary, and today Glacier is home to the most intact complement of native wildlife found anywhere in the contiguous United States.

The diversity of Glacier's wildlife is part of its powerful appeal and an indication of ecosystem health. Diversity is measured by both variety and quantity. By either criterion, this national park seems a success. But preserving a park does not guarantee a future for park wildlife. Their habitat within the park is protected, but they must share it with over 2 million visitors each year. These natural plant and animal communities are also part of larger political and economic communities where human residents need to make a living. The future of these native animals can only be secured through continued cooperation and active guardianship.

◁ *T*he mountain lion's nature is solitary.
Male lions may stake out territories of 175
square miles. Females give birth to a litter of two
or three kittens about every two years. Visitors to
Glacier have a unique opportunity to observe
wild animals living "in a state of nature" filling
their roles in a natural community as predators
and prey.

_S_teller's jays live year-round in ▷
the park where they nest in the
coniferous forests.

◁ *G*lacier is grizzly
country. Hundreds of
the great bears still
roam this wilderness.
Their varied diet
consists mainly of
roots, berries, insects,
and small mammals
like ground squirrels.
Adult grizzly bears
may weigh 350
pounds or more, and
when they stand on
their hind legs for a
better look around they
tower over six feet.
Grizzlies are fast
runners. They can
cover the length of a
football field in less
than six seconds. Park
visitors have a
responsibility to learn
the rules of safe
behavior when they
enter bear country.
Park regulations are
designed to protect
people and to ensure
the survival of this
threatened animal.

27

LORRI L. FRANZ

***T*he mountain lion or**
cougar uses surprise and power to prey on deer, a preferred food. Cougars will also stalk and kill small mammals like beaver and larger ones like elk. In recent years cougars have been more commonly seen in Glacier. Visitors should always exercise caution when they enter the domain of large predators.

◀ ***G*ray wolves have returned**
to Glacier after a 50-year absence. In 1986 a litter of wolf pups was born near the North Fork of the Flathead River. Today over 30 wolves inhabit the north woods of the park.

Predators and Prey

GLENN VAN NIMWEGEN

ERWIN & PEGGY BAUER

A *hoary marmot with a* ▲
*mouthful of dry grass is probably
lining a burrow for winter
hibernation. These residents of
Glacier's alpine meadows are
food for golden eagles and
grizzly bears.*

MICHAEL H. FRANCIS

◀ **R***iver otters spend their*
*lives catching fish from fast-
moving streams. Webbed feet
and thick durable fur equip them
for their watery lifestyle. Otters
are active throughout the year.
They seem to enjoy sledding
down a snow-covered creekbank
no matter what the temperature.*

Wintering Wildlife

ERWIN & PEGGY BAUER

◁ **The wolverine has a fierce** reputation. This effective carnivore travels easily across the snow feeding on porcupines and scavenging for winter-killed animals. Icy crusts and deep snow may strand deer leaving them vulnerable to this aggressive predator.

MICHAEL H. FRANCIS

▲ **Large feet and protective coloring** help snowshoe hares escape predators and survive the winter. In summer the hare's coat changes to light brown.

ED COOPER

◁ **Each winter bighorn sheep migrate to** lower elevations to graze on cured grasses beneath the blanketing snow. As snow melts in the spring, the sheep return to their summer range in mountain meadows. Bighorns are protected from winter's icy blasts by their fat reserves and by a double-layered coat of fine wool covered with hollow insulating hairs. Despite these adaptations, a long hard winter can claim half the lambs born the previous summer.

△ Bull moose paw through the snow to reach shrubs for winter browse. Branches, twigs, and even spruce needles complete their meager winter diet. Healthy moose easily survive long winters if they can find adequate food, but weakened moose are vulnerable to the killing cold.

A young mountain ▷ goat wears a thick winter coat. This yearling will live year-round on high rocky ledges where winter winds expose food plants like heather, lichen, and arctic willow.

▲ **The story of Glacier's wildlife is one of variety, unrivaled in North America. Vernon Bailey, Chief** *Naturalist for the Bureau of Biological Survey, explored the park during the summer of 1917 and observed, "The bird and mammal life of the park are too rich and varied to be touched upon lightly, and each is worthy of a volume by itself. In few other places on the continent can so great a variety of the larger game animals be found close together...while many of the smaller mammals furnish constant interest along the trails." Park visitors who linger here will observe native animals living just as they did in the first decade of park establishment. Bighorn sheep still graze the mountain meadows. This magnificent ram will live to be 12 years of age or more.*

So Great a Variety

◁ **O**ver 30,000 sharp quills protect a porcupine from most predators. Porcupines are at home in the forest where they feed on the bark of pines and firs.

Badgers are residents of grassland and ▲ prairie. They use their sharp powerful claws to excavate their burrows and to dig out small rodents like ground squirrels for food.

◁ **A**s their name implies, Columbian ground squirrels cannot climb trees. These squirrels live in burrows wherever grasses and wildflowers provide abundant food. Ground squirrels live over half their lives in hibernation, a response to a seasonal food supply.

LARRY BURTON

ERWIN & PEGGY BAUER

Mountains of Flowers

▲ **The familiar red Indian paintbrush also occurs** *in hues of white, pink, and orange.*

The endemic Jones columbine ▲ *grows only in the high alpine of Glacier National Park and the mountains of British Columbia.*

▽ **Succulent stonecrop survives on dry** *rocky soils because its thick waxy leaves slow evaporation.*

PAT O'HARA

KATHY AHLENSLAGER

▲ **Alpine talus slopes are home to moss campion,** *a slow-growing cushion plant. A single cushion of moss campion may grow for ten summers before producing its first flower.*

GLENN VAN NIMWEGEN

▲ **R**are mountain lady slipper orchids grow in *the shady understory of mature forests.*

NEAL & MARY JANE MISHLER

▲ **G**illardia or blanketflower colors *the palette of prairie wildflowers.*

CHARLES GURCHE

▲ **T**he edible bulbs of glacier lilies are a favorite *food of grizzly bears. These flowers are the first to bloom as snowbanks recede.*

KATHY AHLENSLAGER

NEAL & MARY JANE MISHLER

◀ **S**hooting *stars bloom in spring at low elevations, but will not flower until late summer in the mountains.*

◀ **C**alypso orchids, also called fairy slippers, are *among the park's 18 different species of orchids.*

35

Waterton Lakes National Park

Waterton Lakes National Park protects 153,600 acres in southern Alberta, Canada. The Canadian government established the park in 1895, 15 years before Glacier would achieve similar status in the United States. Canada and the United States expanded the national park concept in 1932, when they formed Waterton-Glacier International Peace Park, the first to span an international border and a tangible symbol of peace and friendship between two nations.

Although an international boundary divides these two great national parks, Glacier and Waterton function as one natural ecosystem. Water and air flow freely in both directions across the border. Eagles, bears, and wolves use parts of both parks in their annual cycles of migration, hibernation, and searches for food. The United Nations has recognized the significance of both parks by designating them Biosphere Reserves for research, education, and the preservation of biological diversity.

ED COOPER

IRENE HINKE-SACILOTTO

◁ **Blakiston Falls takes its** name from the highest peak in Waterton Lakes National Park. Blakiston Mountain reaches 9,581 feet. When Thomas Blakiston, a member of the British North American Exploring Expedition, came here in 1858, neither Canada nor the United States had surveyed this rugged part of the Rocky Mountains. Official surveys of the international boundary, the 49th parallel, awaited the arrival of the American Northwest Boundary Survey in 1860 and the British Survey Expedition in 1861.

▲ *The view south from Waterton Townsite looks down Upper Waterton Lake and across the* international boundary. Visitors to Waterton can board an excursion boat called the "International," and arrive in Glacier after a short leisurely cruise on the deepest lake in the Canadian Rockies.

The crystal-clear ▷
water of Cameron
Lake spans the
border between
Waterton and Glacier.
Rangers and wardens
from both parks
cooperate to patrol
the wild backcountry
of the International
Peace Park. Park
interpreters from
Glacier and Waterton
lead visitors on
guided hikes across
the international
boundary.

NEAL & MARY JANE MISHLER

ED COOPER

Northern Neighbor

Waterton Lakes is known ▷
as the park "Where the Prairie
Meets the Mountains." As visitors
approach from the east, the
Canadian Rockies and Vimy Ridge
rise abruptly from the plains below.

ERWIN & PEGGY BAUER

▲ **L**upine flowers carpet the
prairie each summer near the
entrance to Waterton Lakes.

▲ **R**ed argillite, a metamorphic siltstone, colors the
walls of Red Rock Canyon in Waterton Lakes National Park.
Both Waterton and Glacier national parks share a common
history of exploration, a diversity of wildlife, and even the
same colorful rock formations. Two hiking trails begin at Red
Rock Canyon, part of over 100 miles of trail in Waterton.

A doe mule deer pauses ▷
along the trail in Waterton. She
uses her large ears to locate a
sound in the lush conifer forest.
Mule deer share the park with
three other species of deer
including elk or wapiti, white-
tailed deer, and moose.

39

Playground and Preserve

Over 800 miles of trail beckon adventurous visitors. Historic hotels and modern highways enable access to Waterton-Glacier International Peace Park. The peace park is the creation of people, but the ecosystem it encompasses cannot be created, only preserved. The native plants and animals of Glacier and Waterton have witnessed a human history of Indians from the plateau and the plains, Hudson Bay trappers, hard scrabble miners, railroad entrepreneurs, loggers, vacationers, and ecologists. The national park idea incorporates the sometimes contradictory goals of both preservation and use. Conflicts and controversy must yield to cooperation and compromise in order to preserve this unique North American experience for the enjoyment of future generations of people from all nations.

The Many Glacier △ Hotel, completed in 1915, was part of a system of hotels, camps, and backcountry chalets built by the Great Northern Railway to encourage travelers to "See America First." Today the hotel is one of five chalets and lodges preserved as National Historic Landmarks.

LAURENCE B. AIUPPY

▲ **R**angers help visitors interpret the park's natural and cultural resources through a varied program of guided hikes, children's activities, and evening campfire talks.

KATHY AHLENSLAGER

▲ **S**ymbols of the International Peace Park, the flags of Canada and the United States fly at Logan Pass Visitor Center located at the high point of the Going-to-the-Sun Road.

Against ▷ the backdrop of the Garden Wall, a cross-country skier enjoys winter, Glacier's quiet time. Less than five percent of park visitors come in winter.

GEORGE WUERTHNER

◁ **M**ist from the *Weeping Wall refreshes bicyclists along Going-to-the-Sun Road. This historic road through the heart of Glacier National Park was completed in 1932.*

People at Play

◁ **H**ikers on the trail to *Hidden Lake experience the alpine beauty of Glacier National Park. Over one-third of the park is alpine. The short summer growing season and thin soils of this community make it vulnerable to the impact of thousands of hikers. The boardwalk linking Logan Pass Visitor Center and the Hidden Lake Overlook was constructed to encourage hikers to stay on this popular trail, to allow the fragile alpine meadows to recover from years of overuse.*

KATHY AHLENSLAGER

△ **O**ver one-half of park visitors go hiking. This trail along Waterton Lake passes through forests of spruce and fir.

RUSS FINLEY

△ **T**he park concessioner maintains a fleet of historic "jammer" buses for tours of the Going-to-the-Sun Road. These carefully maintained buses have been serving park visitors since the 1930s.

SALVATORE VASAPOLLI

A youngster looks △ ▷ on during North American Indian Days held each July in nearby Browning, Montana, on the Blackfeet Reservation. Dance exhibitions, traditional stick games, a parade, and a rodeo highlight this public event.

SALVATORE VASAPOLLI

43

ED COOPER

▲ **Western red cedars frame a portrait of Lake** McDonald near the village of Apgar, one of the earliest settlements in the park.

Glacier Natural History Association

The GNHA manages park bookstores and develops publications to educate visitors about the natural and cultural features of the park. Junior Ranger programs, award-winning trail leaflets, interpretive exhibits, and scholarships to Glacier Institute Field Seminars are but a sample of its important contributions. The association has expanded to include the performing arts as a way to better understand our cultural heritage. Throughout the summer it sponsors performances by Blackfeet storytellers and a one-man show featuring the life and work of western artist Charlie Russell.

SUGGESTED READING

AHLENSLAGER, KATHLEEN E. *Glacier: The Story Behind the Scenery.* Las Vegas, Nevada: KC Publications, 1988.

BUCHHOLTZ, C. W. *Man in Glacier.* West Glacier, Montana: Glacier Natural History Association, 1976.

DIETTERT, GERALD A. *Grinnell's Glacier: George Bird Grinnell and Glacier National Park.* Missoula, Montana: Mountain Press Publishing Company, 1992.

RAUP, OMER B., ROBERT L. EARHART, JAMES W. WHIPPLE, AND PAUL E. CARRARA. *Geology Along the Going-to-the-Sun Road.* West Glacier, Montana: Glacier Natural History Association, 1983.

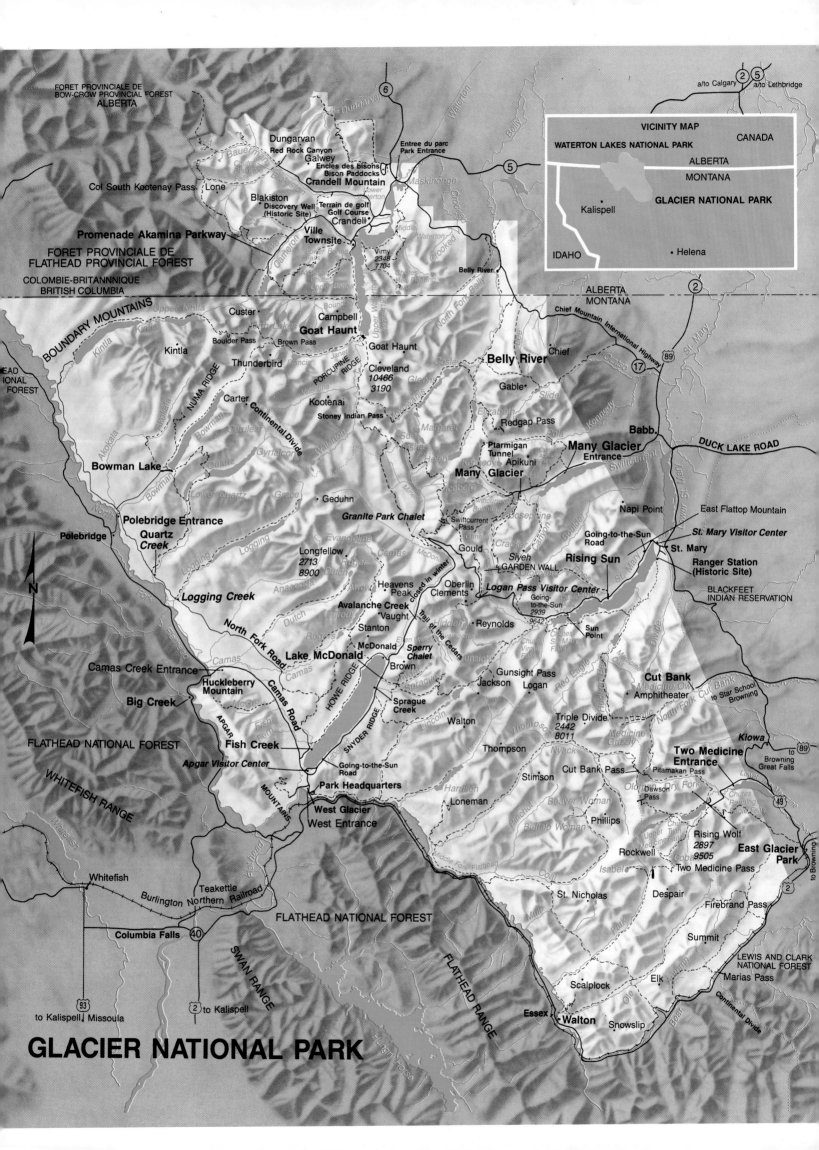

GLACIER NATIONAL PARK

FORET PROVINCIALE DE BOW-CROW PROVINCIAL FOREST
ALBERTA

Dungarvan
Red Rock Canyon
Galwey
Encles des bisons
Bison Paddocks
Crandell Mountain

Col South Kootenay Pass
Lone

Blakiston
Discovery Well
(Historic Site)
Terrain de golf
Golf Course
Crandell

Promenade Akamina Parkway
Ville Townsite

FORET PROVINCIALE DE FLATHEAD PROVINCIAL FOREST
COLOMBIE-BRITANNNIQUE
BRITISH COLUMBIA

Entree du parc
Park Entrance

Vimy
2348
7704

Belly River

VICINITY MAP
WATERTON LAKES NATIONAL PARK
CANADA
ALBERTA
MONTANA
GLACIER NATIONAL PARK
Kalispell
Helena
IDAHO

ALBERTA
MONTANA

BOUNDARY MOUNTAINS

Upper Kintla
Custer
Campbell
Goat Haunt
Chief Mountain International Highway

Kintla
Boulder Pass
Brown Pass
Goat Haunt
Chief
Belly River

Thunderbird
PORCUPINE RIDGE
Cleveland
10466
3190
Gable

NUMA RIDGE
Carter
Continental Divide
Kootenai
Stoney Indian Pass
Redgap Pass

Bowman Lake

Ptarmigan Tunnel
Apikuni
Many Glacier Entrance

Babb.

DUCK LAKE ROAD

Polebridge Entrance
Quartz Creek
Geduhn
Granite Park Chalet
Swiftcurrent Pass
Many Glacier

Napi Point
East Flattop Mountain

Polebridge

Gould
Siyeh
GARDEN WALL
Going-to-the-Sun Road
St. Mary Visitor Center
St. Mary

Longfellow
2713
8900

Logging Creek
Heavens Peak
Oberlin
Clements
Logan Pass Visitor Center
Rising Sun
Ranger Station
(Historic Site)

BLACKFEET INDIAN RESERVATION

Avalanche Creek
Vaught
Trail of the Cedars
Reynolds
Going-to-the-Sun
2939
9642
Sun Point

North Fork Road
Stanton

Lake McDonald
McDonald
Sperry Chalet
Brown

Camas Creek Entrance
Huckleberry Mountain

Gunsight Pass
Jackson
Logan

Cut Bank
Amphitheater
to Star School
Browning

Big Creek
Camas Road
Sprague Creek

FLATHEAD NATIONAL FOREST
Fish Creek
SNYDER RIDGE
Walton

Triple Divide
2442
8011

Kiowa
to Browning
Great Falls

Apgar Visitor Center
Going-to-the-Sun Road

Thompson

Two Medicine Entrance
Pitamakan Pass

Park Headquarters

Stimson
Cut Bank Pass
Dawson Pass

WHITEFISH RANGE

HOWE RIDGE

West Glacier
West Entrance

Loneman

Phillips

East Glacier Park

Whitefish
Teakettle
Burlington Northern Railroad

Harrison

Rising Wolf
2897
9505

Rockwell
Two Medicine Pass

Columbia Falls
40

SWAN RANGE

St. Nicholas
Despair
Firebrand Pass

to Kalispell Missoula
2 to Kalispell

FLATHEAD NATIONAL FOREST

FLATHEAD RANGE

Summit

LEWIS AND CLARK NATIONAL FOREST

Scalplock
Elk
Marias Pass

Essex
Walton
Snowslip

Continental Divide

GLACIER NATIONAL PARK

CARR CLIFTON

John Muir called Glacier the "best care-killing scenery on the continent." In his book *Our National Parks*, published in 1901, Muir recalled his visit to the Glacier region and advised, "Give a month at least to this precious reserve. The time will not be taken from the sum of your life. Instead of shortening, it will indefinitely lengthen it and make you truly immortal. Nevermore will time seem short or long, and cares will never again fall heavily on you, but gently and kindly as gifts from heaven." Glacier National Park is a gift, one to be savored and one to be treasured, for it can be our gift to future generations. Whether your interests include geology or natural history, wildflowers or wildlife, recreation or solitude, a vacation here will add to the "sum of your life."

Chief Mountain stands as a solitary sentinel on the eastern boundary of Glacier National Park. It is a place of cultural significance for the Blackfeet.

JEFF GNASS

▲ **T**wo moods of Mount Oberlin, an autumn afternoon and a summer storm, speak of change. ▷
The golden leaves of a cottonwood almost obscure the snags left from a 1967 forest fire. The storm clouds rolling through Logan Pass may sprinkle snow on unsuspecting summer visitors. Natural systems like Glacier are ever changing, not static but dynamic. Fire and storm are not bad or good, but a part of the continuum of life.

Published by KC Publications, 3245 E. Patrick Ln., Suite A, Las Vegas, NV 89120.

Inside back cover: *At 8,180 feet* ▷
Mount Oberlin towers over the Going-to-the-Sun Road as it traverses Logan Pass. Photo by Gary Ladd.

Back cover: *The Prince of Wales* ▷
Hotel is centerpiece of the view on Upper Waterton Lake. Photo by Ed Cooper.

Created, Designed and Published in the U.S.A.
Printed by Dong-A Printing and Publishing, Seoul, Korea
Color Separations by Kedia/Kwangyangsa Co., Ltd.